MARYSA STORM

BLACK RABBIT BOOKS

Bolt Jr. is published by Black Rabbit Books
P.O. Box 227, Mankato, Minnesota, 56002.
www.blackrabbitbooks.com
Copyright © 2021 Black Rabbit Books

Michael Sellner, designer; Grant Gould, production designer;
Omay Ayres, photo researcher

All rights reserved. No part of this book may be
reproduced in any form without written permission
from the publisher.

Names: Storm, Marysa, author.
Title: ESP / Marysa Storm.
Other titles: Extrasensory perception
Description: Mankato, Minnesota : Black Rabbit Books, [2021]
Series: Bolt Jr.. a little bit spooky | Includes bibliographical
references and index. | Audience: Ages 6-8 | Audience: Grades
K-1 | Summary: "Invites readers to investigate stories about
ESP through engaging text, vibrant imagery, and clear, simple
graphics"– Provided by publisher.
Identifiers: LCCN 2019035656 (print) | LCCN 2019035657 (ebook)
ISBN 9781623104443 (hardcover) | ISBN 9781644664308
(paperback) | ISBN 9781623104740 (ebook)
Subjects: LCSH: Extrasensory perception–Juvenile literature.
Classification: LCC BF1321 .S87 2021 (print) | LCC BF1321
(ebook) | DDC 133.8–dc23
LC record available at https://lccn.loc.gov/2019035656
LC ebook record available at https://lccn.loc.gov/2019035657

Image Credits

Alamy: Hi-Story, 5; Dreamstime: Oksana Kurnosov, 17; Rolffimages, 10–11; iStock: ecastill0, 11; GeorgePeters, 14–15; Henrik5000, 8–9; iMrSquid, 10; Sergey7777, 1; wacomka, 22–23; Shutterstock: Alex Leo, 3, 24; bannosuke, Cover; Bruce Rolff, 12; CLIPAREA l Custom media, 13; Dzhulbee, 20–21; fizkes, 7; Gorodenkoff, 18–19; Illustration Forest, 6–7; peterschreiber.media, 21; Pixel Embargo, 4

Contents

Chapter 1
A Spooky Story 4

Chapter 2
Strange Stories 10

Chapter 3
Studying
the Stories 14

More Information 22

CHAPTER 1
A Spooky Story

In 1898, a man wrote a book. It was about a ship called the *Titan*. In the book, the ship hit an iceberg. The ship sank. Years later, the *Titanic* set sail. The large ship hit an iceberg. Then it sank! Did the man **predict** it?

predict: to say something will happen in the future

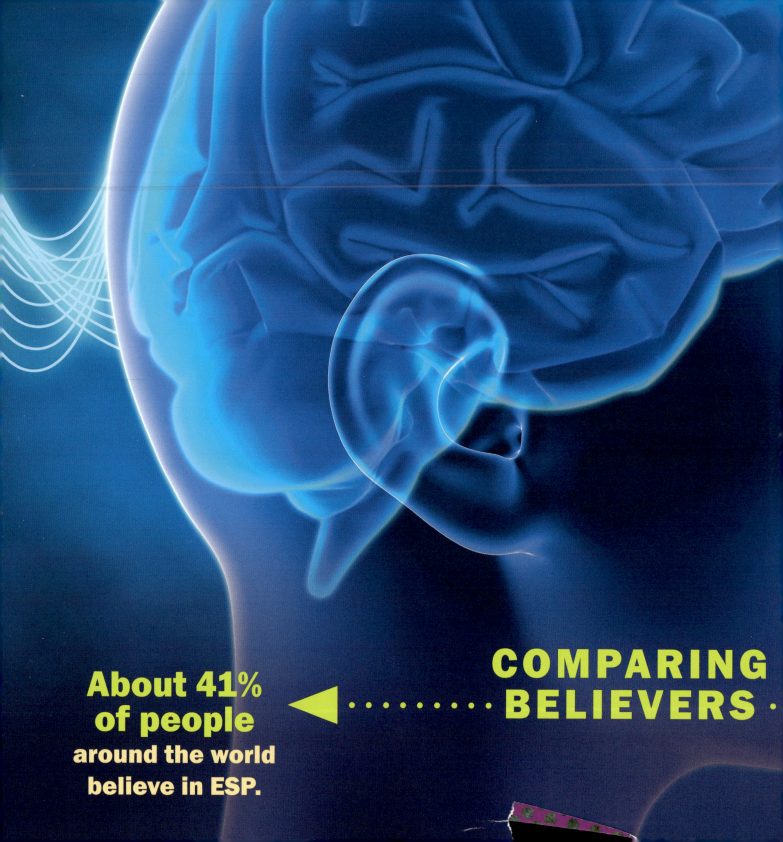

What Is It?

Many stories tell about people seeing the future. These people might have ESP. ESP is like a power. Some people say ESP lets them read minds. Others say they can talk to the dead.

▶ **About 59% of people** around the world don't believe in ESP.

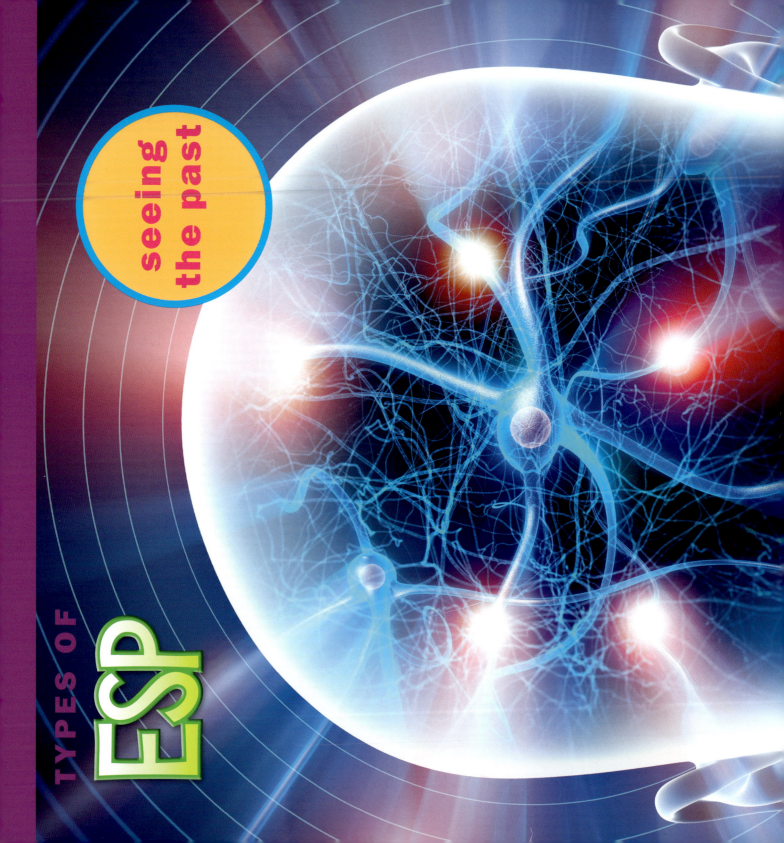

TYPES OF ESP

seeing the past

- seeing the future
- talking to the dead
- reading minds

CHAPTER 2

Strange Stories

There's no proof ESP is real. People tell many stories about it, though. They talk about seeing the future. They see **disasters** before they happen. A mother dreamed a light above her baby fell. She moved the baby. Later, the light fell.

disaster: something that happens suddenly and causes much suffering or loss to many people

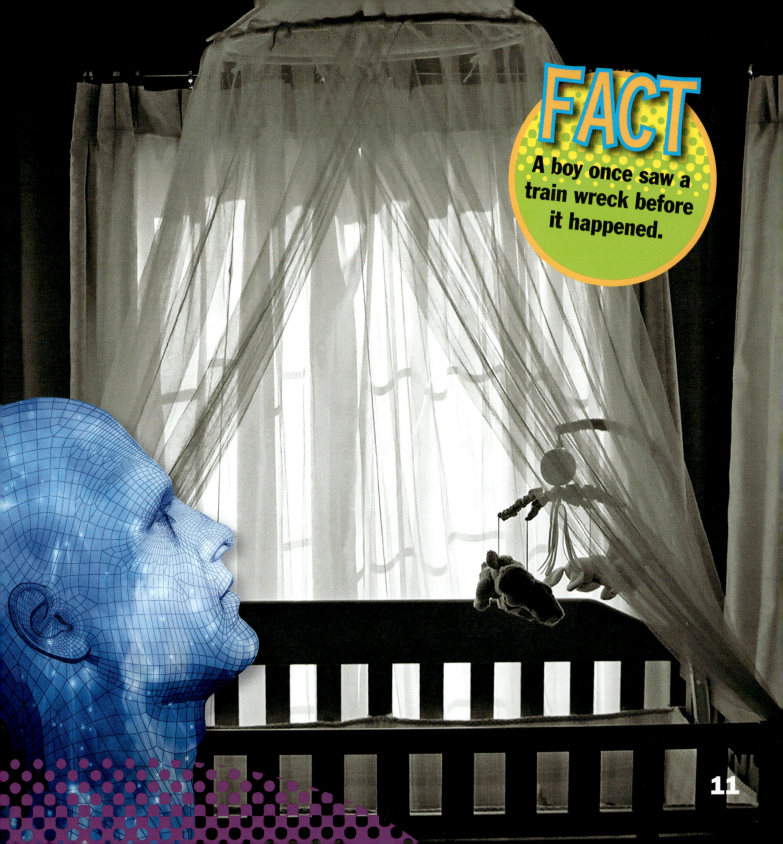

FACT A boy once saw a train wreck before it happened.

11

Helping Out

Believers say ESP can be helpful. They say people have used it to solve **crimes**. Some people helped find bad guys.

crime: activity that is against the law

CHAPTER 3

Studying the Stories

Not everyone believes in ESP. They say people fake having the power. People have made up stories for money.

FACT Some say people faked it for attention.

U.S. Groups Looking for Proof

Independent Investigations Group $100,000 reward for proving ESP is real

California

Texas

For Real?

People have studied ESP. They've asked people to use it in tests. No one has been able to. Some stories are hard to explain, though. Could ESP be real?

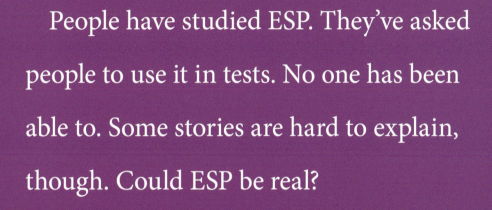

◀ ····· **Only about four percent of scientists believe in ESP.**

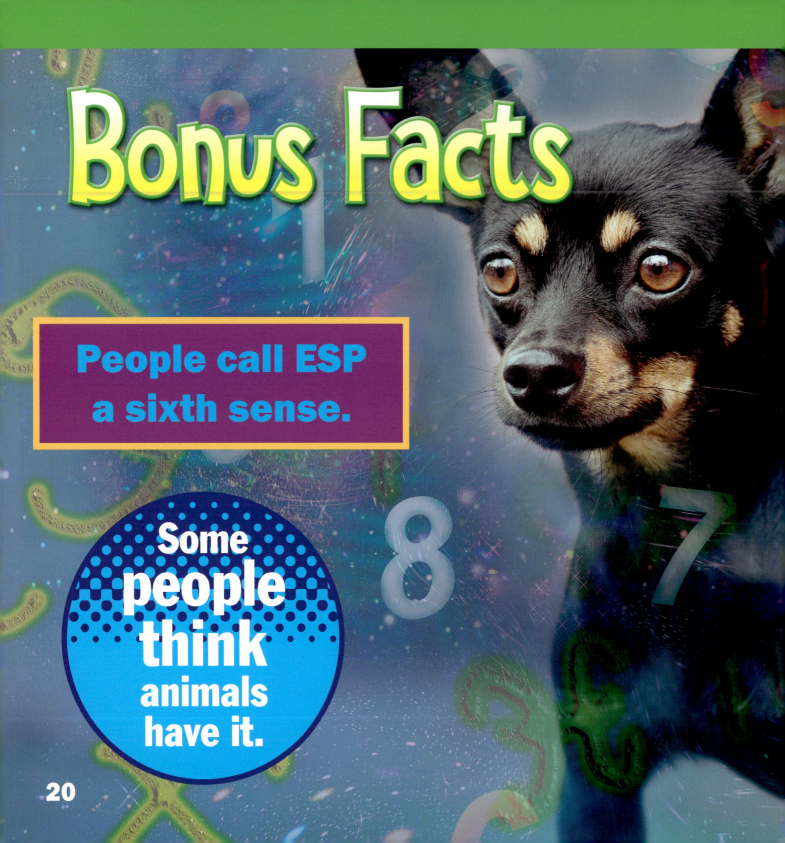

Bonus Facts

People call ESP a sixth sense.

Some people think animals have it.

More people believe in ESP than witches.

More women say they've had psychic experiences than men.

psychic: describes strange mental powers and abilities

READ MORE/WEBSITES

Polinsky, Paige V. *ESP.* Discovery: Investigating the Unexplained. Minneapolis: Bellwether Media, Inc., 2020.

Troupe, Thomas Kingsley. *Extreme Stories about ESP.* That's Just Spooky! Mankato, MN: Black Rabbit Books, 2019.

Do You Have ESP?
wonderopolis.org/wonder/do-you-have-esp

ESP Facts for Kids
easyscienceforkids.com/esp/

The 9 Types of Extrasensory Perception
psychics4today.com/types-extrasensory-perception/

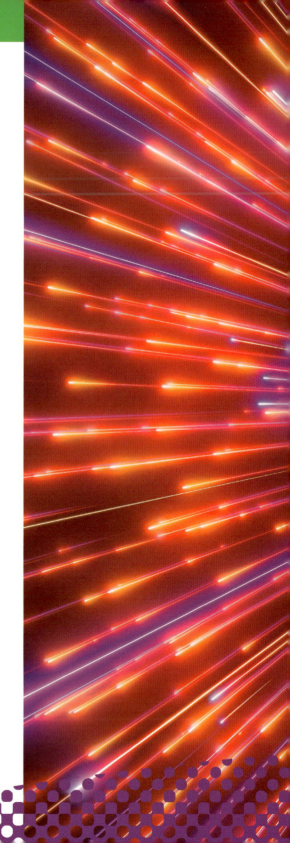

GLOSSARY

crime (KRAHYM)—activity that is against the law

disaster (dih-ZAS-ter)—something that happens suddenly and causes much suffering or loss to many people

predict (pre-DIKT)—to say something will happen in the future

psychic (SI-kik)—describes strange mental powers and abilities

INDEX

K
kinds of ESP, 7, 8–9, 10

P
police cases, 13

R
rewards for proof, 16–17

S
studies, 19